COUNTRY GARDENS
and Other Works for Piano

PERCY GRAINGER

Selected and with an Introduction by
JOSEPH SMITH

DOVER PUBLICATIONS, INC.
Mineola, New York

The editor would like to thank the following for their kind help and interest: Stewart Manville, Don C. Gillespie, John Bird, Barry Peter Ould, Rolf Stang, Stuart Isacoff, and Allan Dameron.

Bibliographical Note

This Dover edition, first published in 2002, is a new compilation of piano works originally published separately in authoritative early editions. Joseph Smith's Introduction was prepared specially for this publication.

Handel in the Strand, Knight and Shepherd's Daughter, and *Blithe Bells* are printed here by the kind permission of The Percy Grainger Estate. *"The Nightingale" and "The Two Sisters"* is reprinted here by permission of The Percy Grainger Estate and Bardic Edition.

Minor engraving errors in *Knight and Shepherd's Daughter* and *March-Jig ("Maguire's Kick")* have been corrected without comment. The footnote on p. 112 is an editorial addition.

International Standard Book Number: 0-486-42241-0

Manufactured in the United States of America
Dover Publications, Inc., 31 East 2nd Street, Mineola, N.Y. 11501

CONTENTS

Molly on the Shore (Irish Reel) (1907)   1

Mock Morris (1910)   16

Irish Tune from County Derry (1911)   26

The Sussex Mummers' Christmas Carol (1911)   32

Colonial Song (1911)   36

Handel in the Strand (Clog Dance, 1911–12)   44

Shepherd's Hey (English Morris Dance Tune, 1908–13)   50

Lullaby from *Tribute to Foster* (1913–15)   58

One More Day, My John (Sea-Chanty, 1915)   76

March-Jig ("Maguire's Kick") (No. 1 of *Four Irish Dances*, 1916)   81

Knight and Shepherd's Daughter (1918)   93

Country Gardens (English Morris Dance Tune, 1918)   98

Spoon River (American Folk-Dance, 1919–22)   104

"The Nightingale" and "The Two Sisters" (1923)   112

Blithe Bells (A free ramble on Bach's aria "Sheep May Safely Graze," 1931)   115

INTRODUCTION

Percy Grainger wrote: "I consider it an affront to destroy a melodiously conceived idea by trying to fit it into the limitations of two hands and a box full of hammers and strings." Although he could play splendidly, and was beloved by the concert-going public, Grainger was a reluctant pianist: performing was a means of underwriting composition, his real love. Naturally, his publishers urged him to capitalize on his reputation as a pianist by making piano versions of works originally intended for other media. He complied, publishing them, programming them, and recording them both on phonograph disks and piano rolls. In his notes to the individual pieces, though, he was always careful to detail the original scoring, for few were originally composed for the piano. Grainger's goal was to retain as much as possible of the contrapuntal content of the original work—whether vocal, chamber, or orchestral—under ten fingers, not to flatter the performer with easy or euphonious "pianistic" textures. Thus, his fascinatingly individual style actually resulted from his *resistance* to the instrument.

I offer no suggestions whatsoever for interpreting the pieces in this new compilation of Grainger's work. After all, Grainger amplifies standard notation with his own idiosyncratic and admirably clear symbols as well as with an abundant scattering of evocative word directions to the player. By these means, he dictates not only every imaginable dynamic nuance and fluctutation of tempo, but also every gradation of pedaling, voicing, and tone color. Perhaps this specificity was related to his scientific attitude toward collecting folksongs: no detail was incidental; every inflection deserved scrupulous notation. It would be madness to add to this wealth—possibly, even excess—of authorial directives and suggestions.

One cannot pin down Grainger to a single nationality: he was born in Australia in 1882, made his name in England, lived most of his life in the United States—he died in White Plains, New York, in 1961—and identified himself as of "Nordic" origin. Pieces included here draw on the folklore, both actual and invented, of these various identities.

British folksong settings remain his best known works, and among these *Country Gardens* was by far the most popular—popular, in fact, even before it was formally "composed." Having enlisted in the United States Army during World War I, Grainger closed some of his "Liberty Loan" concerts (performed in uniform) with an improvisation on this morris-dance tune—invariably to instant acclaim. Since this particular setting originated at the piano, it presents its catchy tune in a form somewhat simpler than Grainger's keyboard transcriptions from other media.

By contrast, *Shepherd's Hey,* another morris-dance setting, abounds in countermelodies. We might not imagine that folksong would readily invite counterpoint. Grainger, however, so internalized the style of the original melodies that he could invent melodic strands in the same style, threading them through the original folk strains. *Shepherd's Hey* is so packed with material that it threatens to explode!

Another Grainger morris dance is *invented* folklore, and thus called *Mock Morris* (on the model, presumably, of "mock turtle" soup).

The first verse of *Irish Tune from County Derry* is a notable example of Grainger's characteristic melody-in-the-middle-of-chords texture. As acknowledged by Grainger himself, Brahms pioneered this style (for example, in his Intermezzo in E-flat, op. 117 no. 1)—but even in Brahms it is unusual, and virtually nonexistent elsewhere in the standard piano repertoire. Grainger professed to espouse this texture because he found it "undemocratic" that the soprano line should so often carry the main tune, with the other voices subservient.

Democracy aside, the richness of the piano's lower register gives a special eloquence to the first statement of *Irish Tune from County Derry*, and to Grainger's similar treatment of *The Sussex Mummer's Christmas Carol*. (Paradoxically, the composer could imbue this carol setting with deep feeling while at times professing himself "rather hostile to the whole gamut of Christian thought and feeling.")

Molly on the Shore is long and fast, and owes much of its special giddiness to repetition. Grainger balances this repetition with more play of tonalities than is usual for him. One effect is unforgettable: having allowed the piece to modulate gradually from G major to F major, he accomplishes the return to G with a sudden, brutal yank.

Grainger was delighted by technological innovations, devoting his last years to inventing machines that could realize his ideal of music unbound by fixed metrical divisions and discrete pitches. Accordingly, he was the first well-known composer to embrace the middle pedal, a late addition to the piano (Steinway started including it around 1874). In many of his pieces, the frequent use of this pedal is an essential element of performance. His spacious, openhearted *Colonial Song* provides explicit examples of every possible tricky use of the middle pedal and its conjunction with the right pedal. Grainger also indicates right-pedal effects with singular care: he cited the lingering, gradated dying away of the final chord as a new effect.

Like his mentor, Edvard Grieg, Grainger was proud to publish settings of folksongs he himself had collected. He collected songs in Denmark with revered veteran Evald Tang Kristensen, and later composed an orchestral *Danish Folk-Music Suite* on the material they had reaped. The work entitled *"The Nightingale" and "The Two Sisters"* is a piano setting of a movement from this suite, incorporating the two folksongs named in the title. Both deal with the supernatural: the first tells of a maiden turned into a nightingale by a spell, then freed by a knight; in the second, a woman murders her younger sister, but the victim succeeds posthumously in revealing the crime.

Grainger collected *Knight and Shepherd's Daughter* in Lincolnshire. The key signature of his setting correctly reflects the modality of the tune—the piece is not in E minor, but E dorian.

The composer's intention that *One More Day, My John* be played in any key as a prelude to another piece reflects a larger principle: his belief that a piece of music should be adaptable to practical circumstances rather than be hermetically confined to a single "pure" form. This principle resulted in his composing ensemble works for "elastic scoring": the conductor is invited to adapt the scoring to any instrumental forces at hand, as long as he preserves the balance between voices.

The notation of the *Lullaby from "Tribute to Foster"* is exceptionally compulsive even for Grainger: he reproduces his piano-roll performance with microscopic precision. Do not despair on seeing the overwhelming snowstorm of little notes. On consulting his instructions, we learn that the filigree figures may be played freely, rather than exactly as notated. The lullaby courts dreaminess through the faint, unmetered buzz of repeating figures, the slow, fluctuating tempo, and the vague paraphrase of Foster's melody.

A Captain Charles H. Robinson heard a fiddler play "Spoon River" at a square dance in 1857. Over half-a-century later—following the publication of Edgar Lee Masters' toughminded *Spoon River Anthology* in 1915—the captain sent a copy of the fiddle tune to Masters; he in turn passed it on to his friend Grainger. Percy dedicated his blunt, determined setting of 1922 to Masters—but that was not quite the end of the interchange.

Two years later, in the opening poem of *The New Spoon River* (a sequel), Masters imagines Captain Robinson speaking from the grave, impressed that ". . . the tune 'Spoon River', played by the nameless fiddler, heard by me as a youth in the evenings of fifty-seven . . ." was transformed "under the genius hands of Percy Grainger."

Two pieces in this collection are re-compositions of works by other composers, including Bach, one of Grainger's favorites. (Bach's Organ Fugue in A Minor, in Liszt's piano transcription, is one of Grainger's most distinguished recordings.) *Blithe Bells* is based on Bach's famous aria "Sheep May Safely Graze." Grainger's version differs from the original *only* in regard to tonality, rhythm, form, harmony, meter, and texture! While any transcription tends to rob the original of its tone colors, the question is whether it gives anything worthwhile in return. *Blithe Bells* in fact offers something utterly new: a delicate impressionistic study. The passages in tenths, while rendering the piece impossible for small hands, produce an enchanting jingling.

The other re-composition, *March-Jig ("Maguire's Kick"),* is actually a third-degree adaptation. Charles Villiers Stanford is remembered as both composer and teacher (Ralph Vaughan Williams was one of his students). Stanford based his *Four Irish Dances* for piano on tunes from the legendary *Petrie Collection of the Ancient Music of Ireland* (1855)—the source, as well, for Grainger's *Irish Tune from County Derry*. Stanford then orchestrated the dances, and Grainger arranged *those* orchestral dances for piano. *Maguire's Kick* makes occasional use of crossed hands and rapidly alternating hands—the kind of showy techniques that are virtually absent from Grainger's transcriptions of his own music.

Although the title *Handel in the Strand* was not coined by Grainger himself, it accurately suggests the breadth of the composer's sympathies. Baroque counterpoint, changing meters, syncopation, modality—and a tune of unabashed, blatant vulgarity—who but Grainger could blend these elements into a satisfying composition? Who else would try? As man and musician, Percy Grainger quite transcends classification. He liked the things he liked . . . and they were disparate.

Happily, there has been an explosion of interest in Grainger in recent years. For those who would like to learn more about him, John Bird's biography remains a classic and is readily available.[1] Two volumes of letters offer the man's fascinating preoccupations and contradictions in his own words.[2,3] But to the musician, the volume *Grainger on Music* is of particular importance in understanding this unique artist's relentless challenges to musical orthodoxy.[4]

JOSEPH SMITH
New York, Fall 2001

The *New York Times* called pianist Joseph Smith's playing "eloquent," and the *Frankfurter Allgemeine Zeitung* found him a "richly sensitive interpreter." His close involvement with the music of Percy Grainger has included live and radio performances, recordings, articles and lectures. Smith was honored to have given first performances of Grainger's *In Dahomey* in New York, San Francisco, and several major European cities. Joseph Smith is author of *Piano Discoveries* (Ekay Music), and editor of *Four Early 20th Century Piano Suites by Black Composers* (G. Schirmer), and *American Piano Classics* (Dover). His articles on piano music have appeared in major periodicals, and his feature "Joseph Smith's Piano Bench" is heard regularly on National Public Radio's *Performance Today*.

---

[1]Bird, John. *Percy Grainger.* New York: Oxford University Press, 1999.

[2]Dreyfus, Kay (ed.). *The Farthest North of Humanness: Letters of Percy Grainger 1901–14.* St. Louis, MO: Magnamusic-Baton, 1985.

[3]Gilles, Malcolm, and David Pear (eds.). *The All-Round Man: Selected Letters of Percy Grainger 1914–16.* New York: Oxford University Press, 1994.

[4]Gillies, Malcolm, and Bruce Clunies Ross (eds.). *Grainger on Music.* New York: Oxford University Press, 1999.

(Lovingly and reverently dedicated to the memory of Edvard Grieg)

Nº 19. "MOLLY ON THE SHORE"

Birthday-gift, Mother, 3.7.'07

IRISH REEL

for

PIANO

Piano setting, April, 1918

"Molly on the shore" was originally set for string four-some or string band (summer 1907) *(Schott & Co., London)*

"Molly on the shore" is also set for symphony orchestra, theatre orchestra, and violin and piano. (Early 1914) *(Schott & Co., London)*

based on two Cork Reel tunes, "Temple hill" and "Molly on the shore", respectively Nos. 901 and 902 of THE COMPLETE PETRIE COLLECTION OF ANCIENT IRISH MUSIC edited by Sir Charles Villiers Stanford (Boosey & Co., London.)

By kind permission of Sir Charles Villiers Stanford

by

PERCY ALDRIDGE GRAINGER

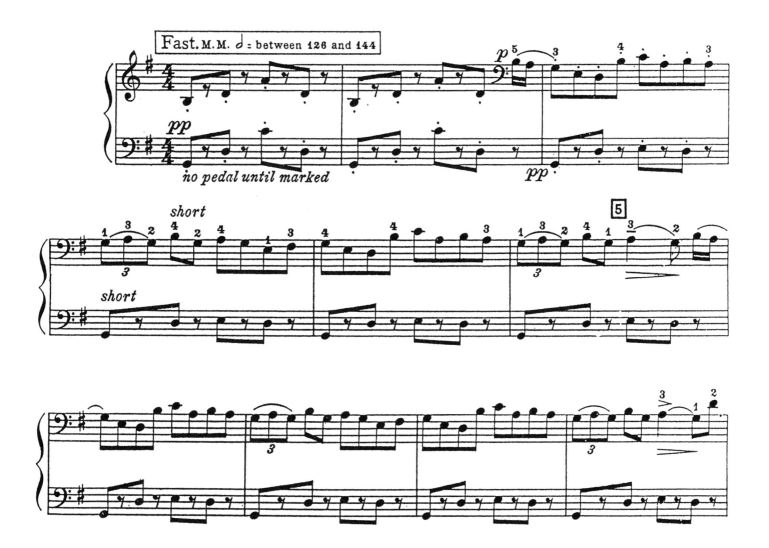

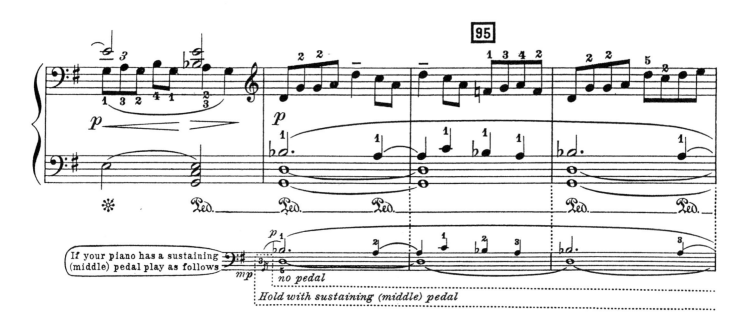

If your piano has a sustaining (middle) pedal play as follows

no pedal

Hold with sustaining (middle) pedal

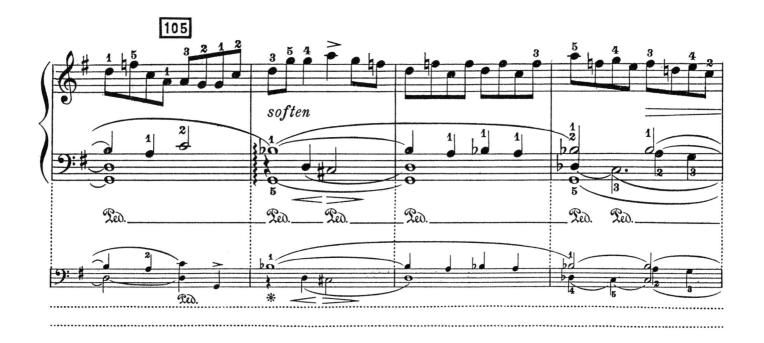

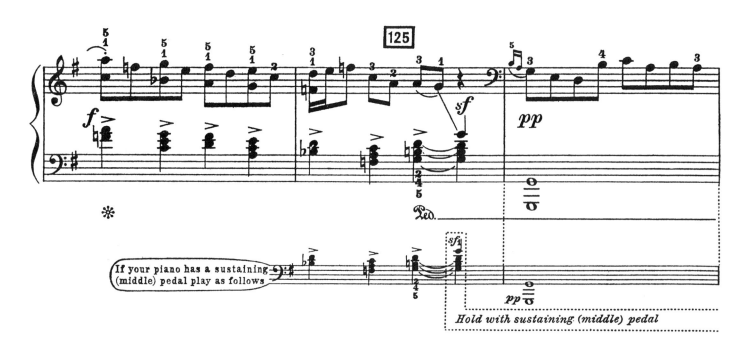

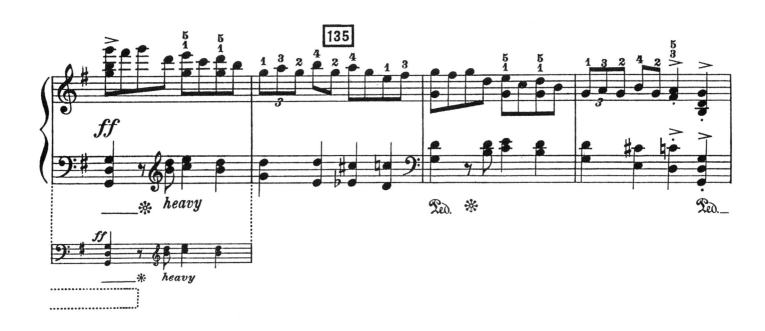

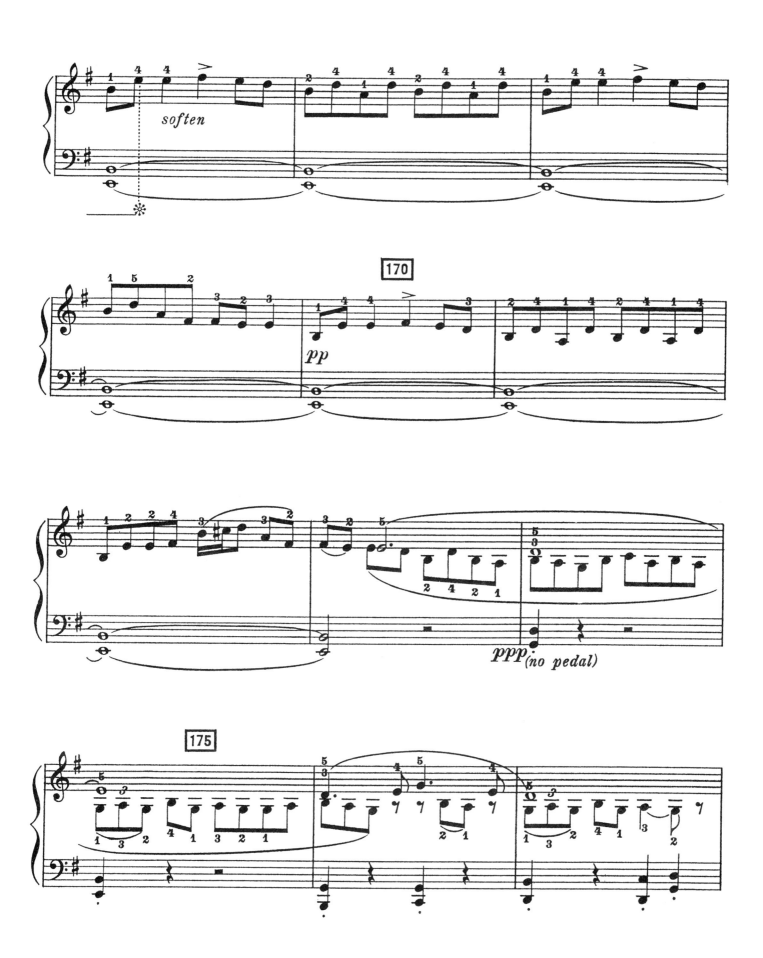

Dished up for piano, April, 1918,
Bayridge, Brooklyn.

No. 1. MOCK MORRIS.

for string six - some (6 single players) or string band
by
PERCY ALDRIDGE GRAINGER.

begun 19.5.1910. | ended 4.6.1910.

No folk - music tune - stuffs at all are used herein. The rhythmic cast of the piece is Morris-like, but neither the build of the tunes nor the general lay - out of the form keeps to the Morris dance shape.
P.A.G.

All held within the above square is meant to be used in full in programs, where possible.

Birthday - gift, Mother. 3.7.10.

For Piano.
Concert version.

*The tune of bars 9, 10, 11 & 12 is (unwittingly) cribbed from an early "Magnificat" of Cyril Scott's. He has used the phrase again in a piano piece "Chimes" op. 40, No. 3, (Elkin & Co. Ltd.) in which it can be consulted. P.A.G.

16

PERCY ALDRIDGE GRAINGER.

BRITISH FOLK-MUSIC SETTINGS.

(Lovingly and reverently dedicated to the memory of Edvard Grieg.)

Nr 6. IRISH TUNE FROM COUNTY DERRY.

(NAME UNKNOWN).

Set for Piano | Begun: October, 1902. | Ended: July, 1911.

The tune was collected by MISS J. ROSS, of New Town, Limavady Co. Derry (Ireland) and

PRINTED IN

"The Petrie Collection of the Ancient Music of Ireland" *(Dublin, 1855)*

on page **57** of which collection the following remarks by GEORGE PETRIE go before the tune, which is headed: "Name unknown":

> "For the following beautiful air I have to express my very grateful acknowledgment to MISS J. ROSS, of New Town, Limavady, in the County of Londonderry— a lady who has made a large collection of the popular unpublished melodies of the county, which she has very kindly placed at my disposal, and which has added very considerably to the stock of tunes which I had previously acquired from that still very Irish county. I say still very Irish, for though it has been planted for more than two centuries by English and Scottish settlers, the old Irish race still forms the great majority of its peasant inhabitants; and there are few, if any counties in which, with less foreign admixture, the ancient melodies of the country have been so extensively preserved. The name of the tune unfortunately was not ascertained by Miss Ross, who sent it to me with the simple remark that it was 'very old,' in the correctness of which statement I have no hesitation in expressing my perfect concurrence."

N⁰ 6. IRISH TUNE FROM COUNTY DERRY,

(NAME UNKNOWN)

Set for Piano by
Percy Aldridge Grainger.

The tune is thro'out printed in bigger notes

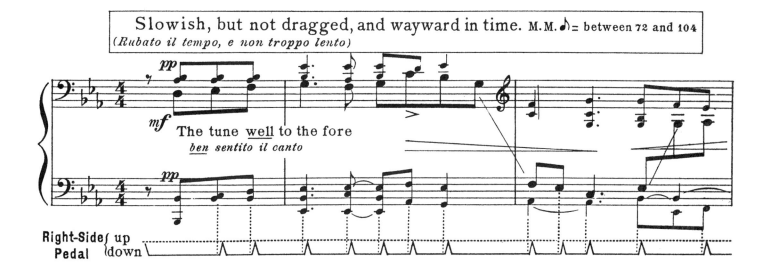

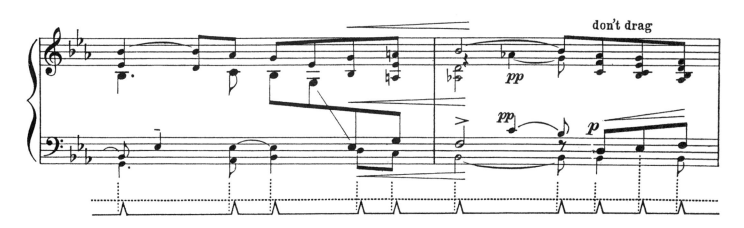

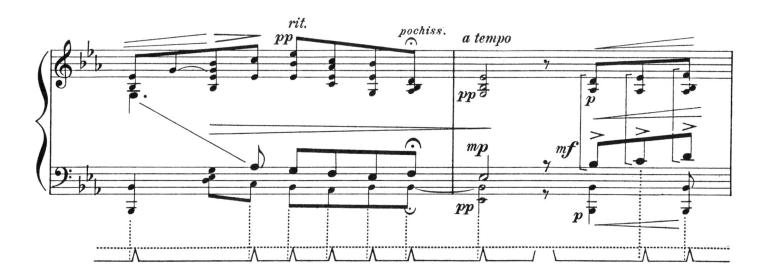

✻ This note (here altered by me) is B♮ in the original. *P. G.*

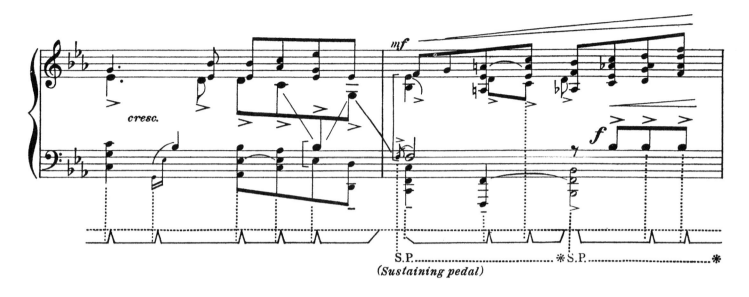

S.P. _____ *S.P. _____ *
(Sustaining pedal)

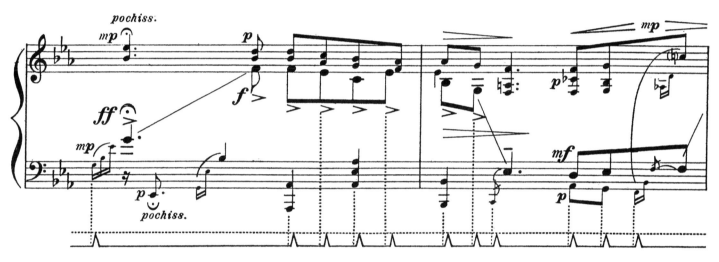

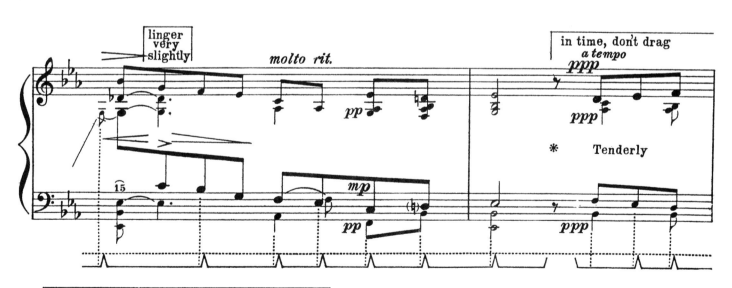

> *If you like, the passage between * and **
> may be played an octave higher (in both hands)

These middle notes well to the fore:
B   A   G   F   E

well to the fore

don't drag; if anything, slightly faster

* This note (here altered by me) is B♮ in the original. *P. G.*

BRITISH FOLK-MUSIC SETTINGS.

(Lovingly and reverently dedicated to the memory of Edvard Grieg.)

N.º 2. THE SUSSEX MUMMERS' CHRISTMAS CAROL.

(By kind permission of Miss Lucy E. Broadwood.)

Set for piano by Percy Grainger. | begun 1905 | ended 1911 |

The tune was noted by Miss Lucy E. Broadwood at Lyne, near Horsham (Sussex), in 1880 and 1881 from the singing of Christmas Mummers called "Tipteers" or "Tipteerers" during their play of "St. George, the Turk, and the seven champions of Christendom."

See: ENGLISH TRADITIONAL SONGS AND CAROLS   *(Boosey & C.º)*

by Lucy E. Broadwood, pp 80 and 122, and

JOURNAL OF THE FOLK-SONG SOCIETY, vol. ii., N.º 7, p 128.

All held within the above square is meant to be used in full in programs, where possible.

The Tune, printed in big notes, should throughout be brought out with a rich piercing tone and heard well above the accompanying parts.

The words sung to the Carol contain, among others, the following verses (which may be used in programs, at will):

> O mortal man, remember well
> When Christ our Lord was born;
> He was crucified betwixt two thieves,
> And crownèd with the thorn.

> O mortal man, remember well
> When Christ died on the rood;
> It was for we and our wickedness
> Christ shed His precious blood.

> God bless the mistress of this house
> With a gold chain round her breast;
> It's whether she sleeps, or whether she wakes,
> Lord send her soul to rest.

> God bless the master of this house
> With happiness beside;
> It's whether he walks, or whether he rides,
> Lord Jesus be his guide.

> God bless your house, your children too,
> Your cattle and your store;
> The Lord increase you day by day,
> And send you more and more.

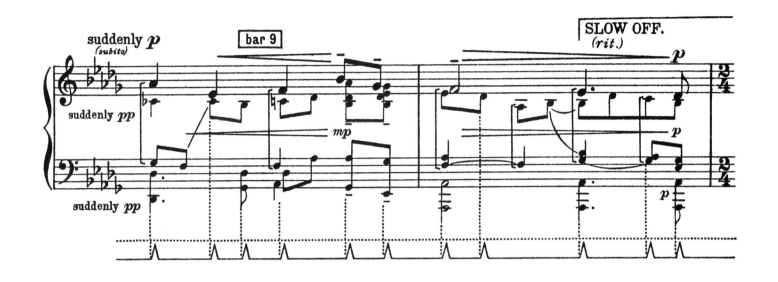

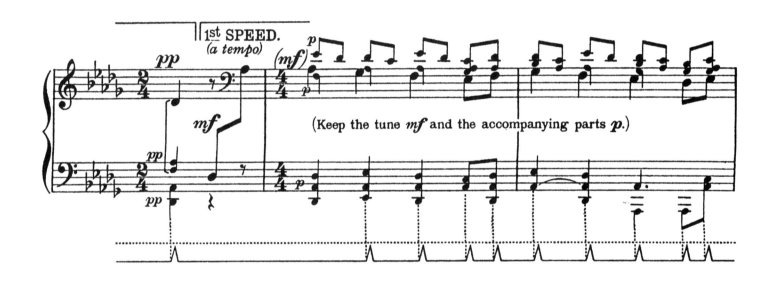

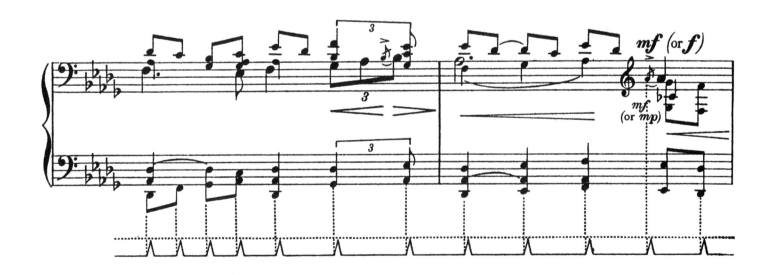

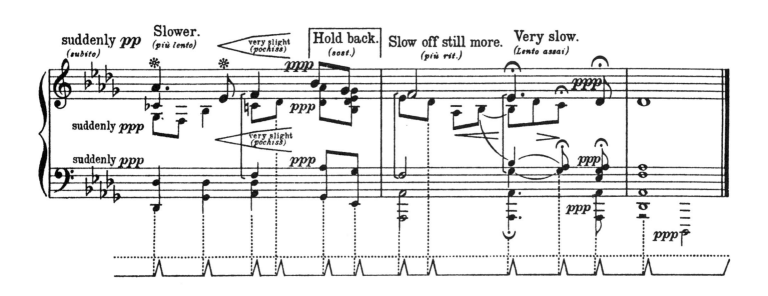

✻ The rhythm of these 2 notes is here altered by me. The original form is given in the first time through [(full) bar 9]. *P. G.*

PERCY ALDRIDGE GRAINGER

SENTIMENTALS

Nº 1. COLONIAL SONG

Originally composed for 2 voices (soprano and tenor), harp and full orchestra.

| Composed as Yule-gift for mother, 1911 | Scored as Yule-gift for mother, 1912 | Rescored, early 1914 |

Short Program Note

In this piece the composer has wished to express feelings aroused by thoughts of the scenery and people of his native land, Australia. It is dedicated to the composer's mother.

Long Program Note

No traditional tunes of any kind are made use of in this piece, in which I have wished to express feelings aroused by thoughts of the scenery and people of my native land, (Australia), and also to voice a certain kind of emotion that seems to me not untypical of native-born Colonials in general.

Perhaps it is not unnatural that people living more or less lonelily in vast virgin countries and struggling against natural and climatic hardships (rather than against the more actively and dramaticly exciting counter wills of their fellow men, as in more thickly populated lands) should run largely to that patiently yearning, inactive sentimental wistfulness that we find so touchingly expressed in much American art; for instance in Mark Twain's "Huckleberry Finn," and in Stephen C. Foster's adorable songs "My Old Kentucky Home," "Old Folks at Home," etc.

I have also noticed curious, almost Italian-like, musical tendencies in brass band performances and ways of singing in Australia (such as a preference for richness and intensity of tone and soulful breadth of phrasing over more subtly and sensitively varied delicacies of expression), which are also reflected here.

Percy Aldridge Grainger

Piano Solo

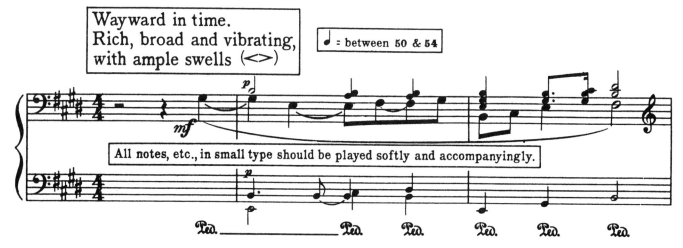

Wayward in time.
Rich, broad and vibrating,
with ample swells (<>)

♩ = between 50 & 54

All notes, etc., in small type should be played softly and accompanyingly.

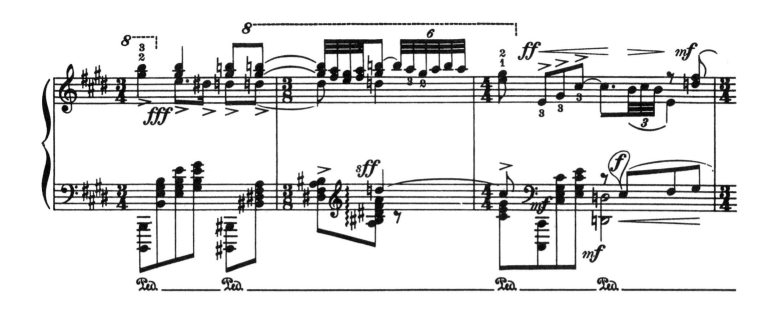

soften
(dim.)

Top notes well to the fore

Gradually quieter and

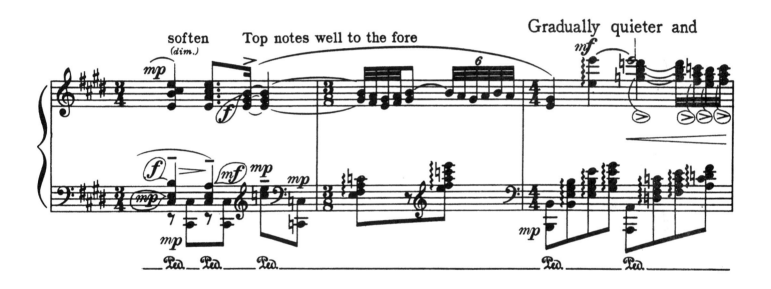

slower

♩ = about 40

gently

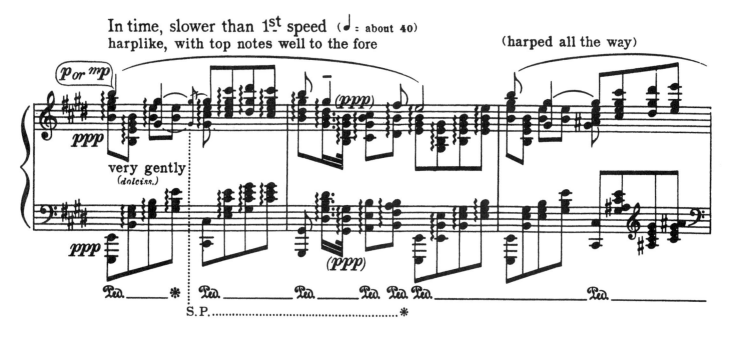

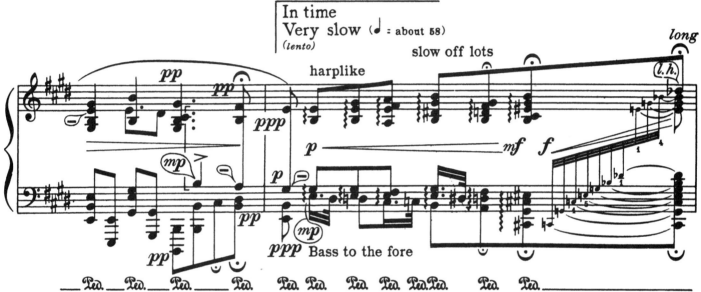

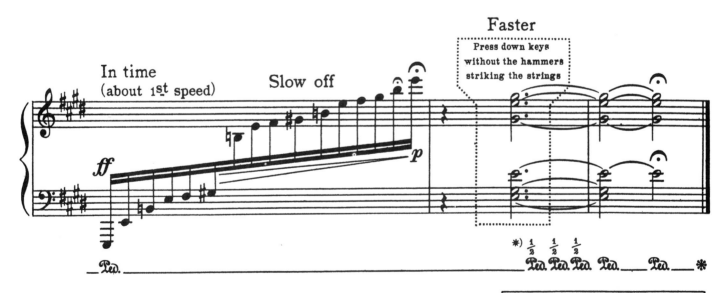

*) By "half pedalling" is meant lifting
up the right foot pedal just so high that
the dampers only partially arrest the
vibrations of the strings.

Colonial Song 43

For my dear friend William Gair Rathbone

Nͦ 2 "HANDEL IN THE STRAND"
CLOG DANCE

Composed for piano
and 2 or more strings
(or for massed pianos
& string orchestra).
Feb., 1911-April 13, 1912.

Dished up for piano
solo, March 25, 1930,
Denton, Texas.

to be played to, or without, clog dancing

by
PERCY ALDRIDGE GRAINGER

Program-note

My title was originally "Clog Dance". But my dear friend William Gair Rathbone
(to whom the piece is dedicated) suggested the title "Handel in the Strand", because
the music seemed to reflect both Handel and English musical comedy (the "Strand"
is the home of London musical comedy). In bars 1 - 16 (and their repetition, bars
47 - 60) I have made use of matter from some variations of mine on Handel's "Har-
monious Blacksmith" tune.   *Percy Aldridge Grainger*

VERSION FOR PIANO SOLO

BRITISH FOLK-MUSIC SETTINGS

(Lovingly and reverently dedicated to the memory of Edvard Grieg)

No. 4

"SHEPHERD'S HEY"

ENGLISH MORRIS DANCE TUNE

| Begun: 1908 | Ended: December, 1913 |

SET FOR PIANO BY PERCY ALDRIDGE GRAINGER
USING 4 VARIANTS

COLLECTED BY

CECIL J. SHARP

From the playing of the fiddler of the Bidford Morris Dancers (1906), J. Mason (Stow on the Wold), W. Hathaway (Cheltenham) and William Wells (Bampton).

Morris Dances are still danced by teams of "Morris Men" decked out with bells and quaint ornaments to the music of the fiddle or "the pipe and tabor" (a sort of drum and fife) in several agricultural districts in England. The tune of "Shepherd's Hey" (which is akin to the North English air "Keel row") is very widely found throughout England. For variants of this and other English Morris Dance tunes see Cecil Sharp's "Morris Dance Tunes" (Novello & Co., Ltd., London). The word "Hey" denotes a particular figure in Morris Dancing. For instructions in how to dance the Morris, and much other interesting information about this important but only recently investigated branch of folk-dancing, consult Cecil Sharp's "The Morris Book" (Novello & Co., Ltd., London).

"Shepherd's Hey"
English Morris Dance Tune

N.B. This setting is not suitable to dance Morris Dances to. All big stretches may be played broken (harped).

Set for piano by
Percy Aldridge Grainger

The bigger printed notes should
be heard well above the others

The top notes as piercing as possible.

*)⁎ **below a note means that the last pedal is to be raised just at the moment of striking the keys and pressed down again as fast as possible.**

*) It does'nt matter exactly what note the glissando ends on.

LULLABY *from* "TRIBUTE TO FOSTER"

FOR PIANO *by* PERCY ALDRIDGE GRAINGER

A study in "musical glasses" effect based upon Stephen Foster's Song "Camptown Races" (also called "Doodah")

Loving birthday-gifts for mother,
July 3d, 1914, and July 3d, 1916.

"Tribute to Foster" for solo voices, chorus and orchestra,
begun in the spring of 1913.

Piano piece worked out summer of 1915 in New York City.

One of my earliest musical recollections is that of my mother singing me to sleep with Stephen Foster's song "Camptown Races" ("Doodah").

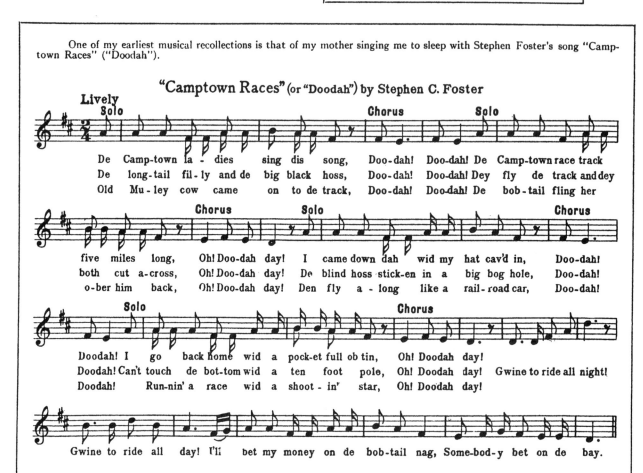

"Camptown Races" (or "Doodah") by Stephen C. Foster

De Camp-town la - dies sing dis song, Doo-dah! Doo-dah! De Camp-town race track
De long-tail fil - ly and de big black hoss, Doo-dah! Doo-dah! Dey fly de track and dey
Old Mu - ley cow came on to de track, Doo-dah! Doo-dah! De bob - tail fling her

five miles long, Oh! Doo-dah day! I came down dah wid my hat cav'd in, Doo-dah!
both cut a-cross, Oh! Doo-dah day! De blind hoss stick-en in a big bog hole, Doo-dah!
o-ber him back, Oh! Doo-dah day! Den fly a - long like a rail- road car, Doo-dah!

Doodah! I go back home wid a pock-et full ob tin, Oh! Doo-dah day!
Doodah! Can't touch de bot-tom wid a ten foot pole, Oh! Doo-dah day! Gwine to ride all night!
Doodah! Run-nin' a race wid a shoot - in' star, Oh! Doo-dah day!

Gwine to ride all day! I'll bet my money on de bob-tail nag, Some-bod-y bet on de bay.

In the spring of 1913 I began a composition for solo voices, chorus and orchestra based on this entrancing ditty, entitled "Tribute to Foster," in which I wished to give musical expression to these Australian memories and to my ever-increasing love and reverence for this great American genius—one of the most tender, touching and subtle melodists and poets of all time; a mystic dreamer no less than a whimsical humorist. It is, maybe, only natural that I should instinctively think of "Camptown Races" both as a dance-song and as a lullaby, and at the beginning and end of my above-mentioned choral composition the tune is heard in its original lively character, while in the middle of the work is interposed a "lullaby" section mirroring a mood awakened by memories of my mother's singing, in which the Foster tune is treated very freely indeed, and in which solo strings, piano, harp, celesta, glockenspiel, Deagan steel marimbaphone or Hawkes' resonaphone (played with bows), Deagan wooden marimbaphone (played with bows), and a large army of wineglasses and glass bowls of greatly varying sizes and pitches (their rims rubbed by wet fingers) accompany six solo voices that sing the following verses of my own:

In Pittsburgh town a man did dwell;
    (Doodah! Doodah!)
His name was Foster as I've heard tell.
    (Oh! Doodah day!)

Foster's dead and gone away;
    (Doodah! Doodah.)
His songs dey lib for eber an' aye.
    (Oh! Doodah day!)

(*Refrain*)
Gwine to still be sung
As long as de worl's heart's young.

Foster's songs weren't Darkie quite;
Yet neither were they merely "white."

Foster's songs dey make you cry;
Bring de tear-drop to yo' eye.

———

Deze songs dey trabble de worl' around;
At las' dey come to Adelaide town.

———

When I was young on my mummy's knee
She sang dat race course song to me.

———

Sang it to me sweet as a lullaby;
Hear dat song till de day I die.

This piano piece is a free paraphrase of the lullaby section, and sets out to reflect, in its twiddly filigree work, something of the almost mesmeric quality of the sound of the "musical glasses" and Deagan instruments.

PERCY ALDRIDGE GRAINGER.

HINTS TO PERFORMERS.

To reproduce upon the piano something of the mesmeric charm of "musical glasses" and bowed Deagan steel and wooden marimbaphones (or Hawkes' resonaphone) the repeated fluttering figures should be played very evenly and with legato pedaling, so as to give an *unbroken rhythm-less* flow of singing sound. Do not try to make each repeating note come out

distinctly in such passages as  on the contrary, try and get a rich *blur* of pedalled sound, with *no individual note sticking out;* no separate blow of the hammer clearly heard. Likewise

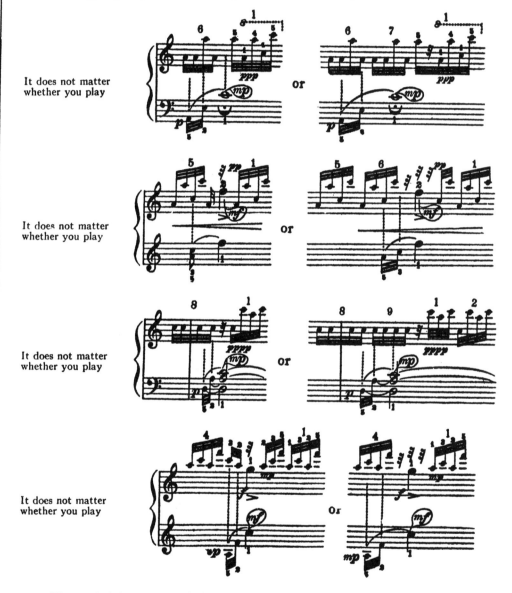

should be sounded as a quickly prattling rush of indistinctly-heard notes, not like clean clear passage-work.

You need not play the joins between the various sections of florid passages note for note as they stand, nor need you follow this copy implicitly as to the exact rhythmic relation between your right and left hands. For instance,

It does not matter whether you play ... or ...

It does not matter whether you play ... or ...

It does not matter whether you play ... or ...

It does not matter whether you play ... or ...

The speed of the passage-work should vary slightly from moment to moment at the discretion of the player, and both hands should play *very waywardly* as to time, and quicken and slacken *independently of each other.* Thus the speed of the fluttering right hand arabesques may be greatened at the same time that the left hand is slowing off, or the left hand quicken while the right slackens.

This Lullaby is a *sound-study* to be solved by each player individualisticly in his or her own way, with plenty of freedom as to expression marks (those printed should be taken merely as hints), swells (< >) and treatment of the twiddly passage-work. This copy is noted down by me from a Duo-Art Pianola record of an actual hand-played performance by me, thereby preserving, as it were photographicly, all the rhythmic irregularities of an individual rendering, and is not intended to be followed slavishly, note for note, by other players.

Percy Aldridge Grainger.

PERCY ALDRIDGE GRAINGER
LULLABY from "Tribute to Foster"

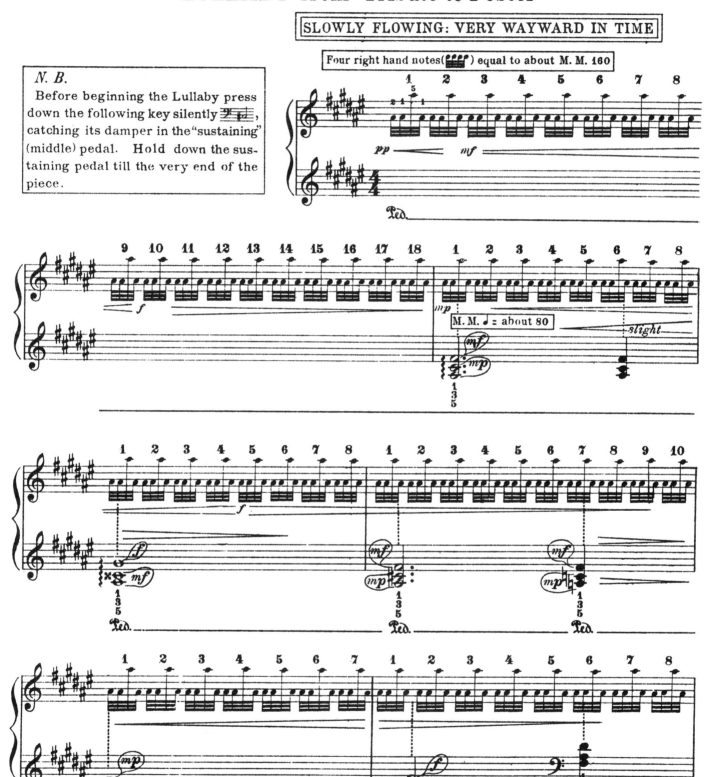

N. B.

Before beginning the Lullaby press down the following key silently, catching its damper in the "sustaining" (middle) pedal. Hold down the sustaining pedal till the very end of the piece.

SLOWLY FLOWING: VERY WAYWARD IN TIME

Four right hand notes equal to about M. M. 160

M. M. ♩ = about 80

QUICKEN SOMEWHAT

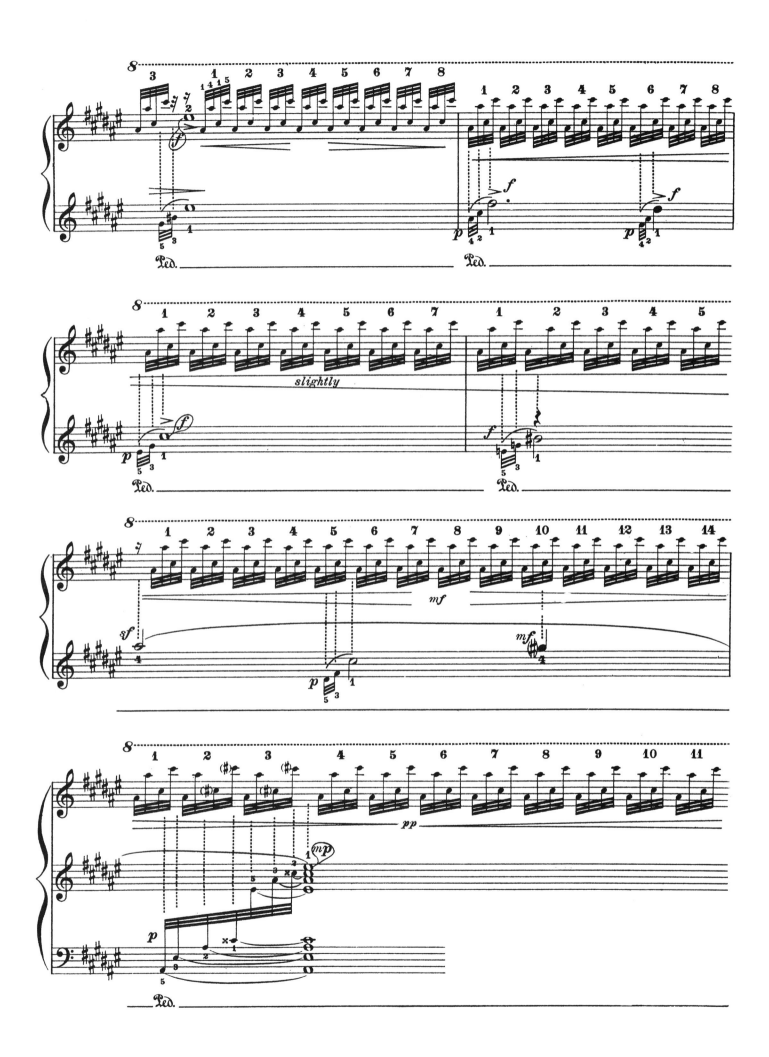

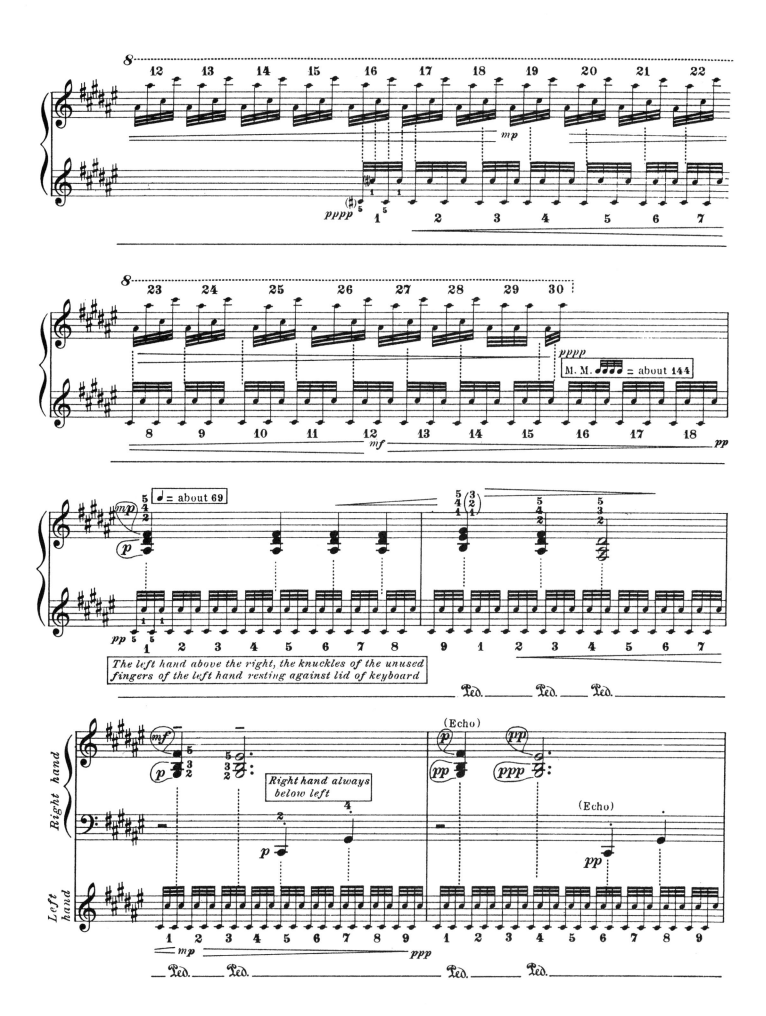

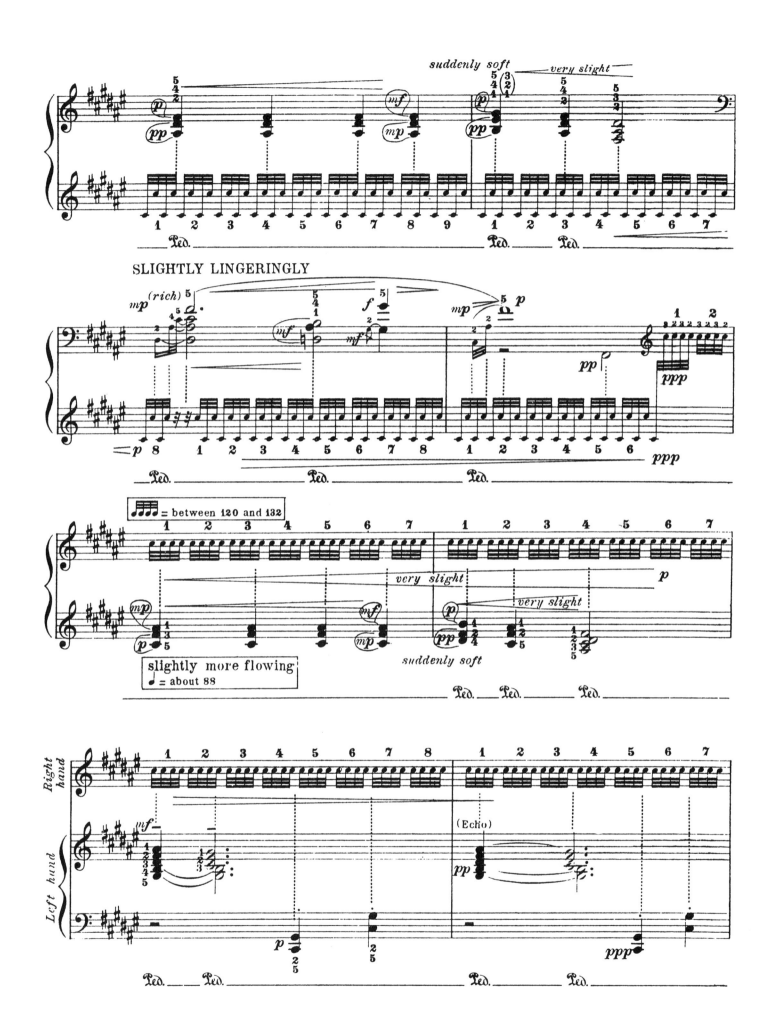

the swells in the right hand should not follow the expression marks of the left hand, but run, oftenest, at cross purposes to them.

quicken very slightly

slow off slightly

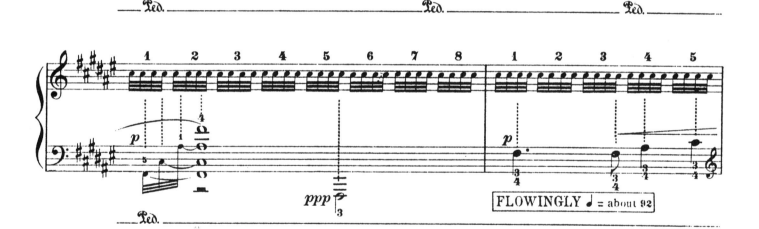

very lingeringly

Rich, like men's voices

FLOWINGLY ♩ = about 92

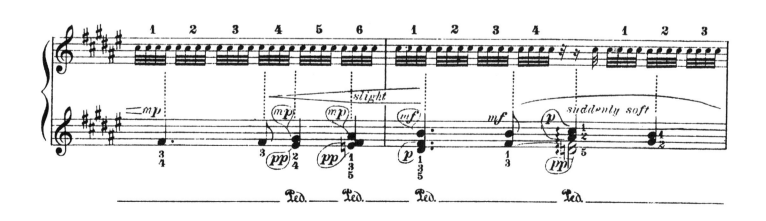

slight

suddenly soft

GRADUALLY SLOWER AND SLOWER

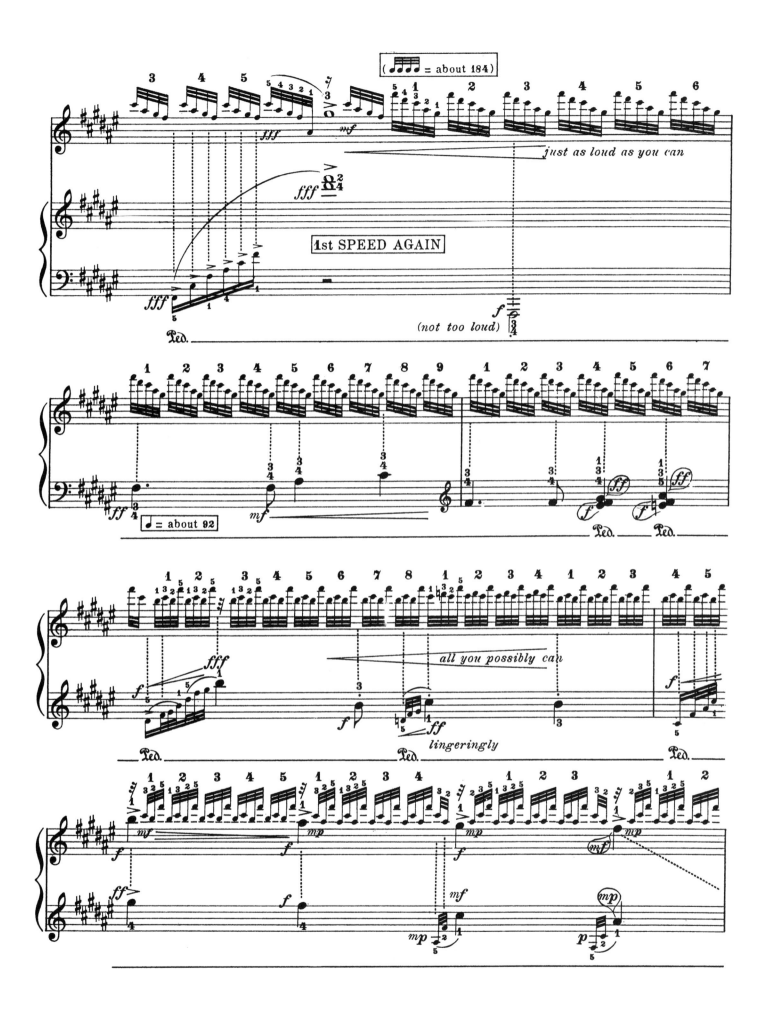

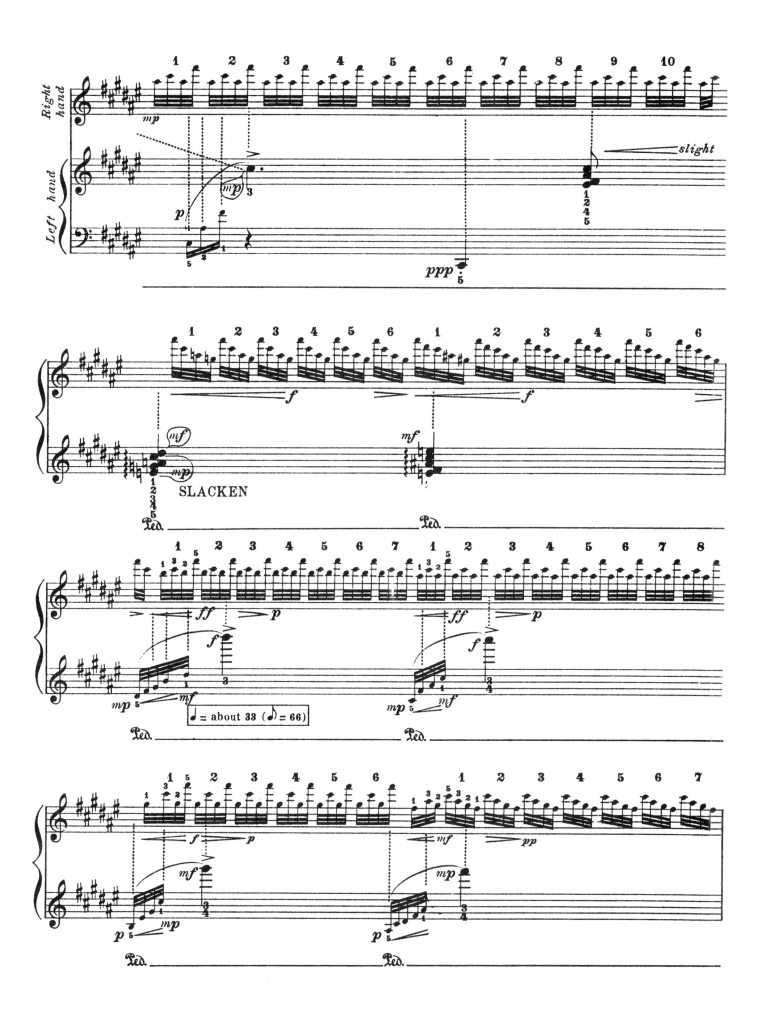

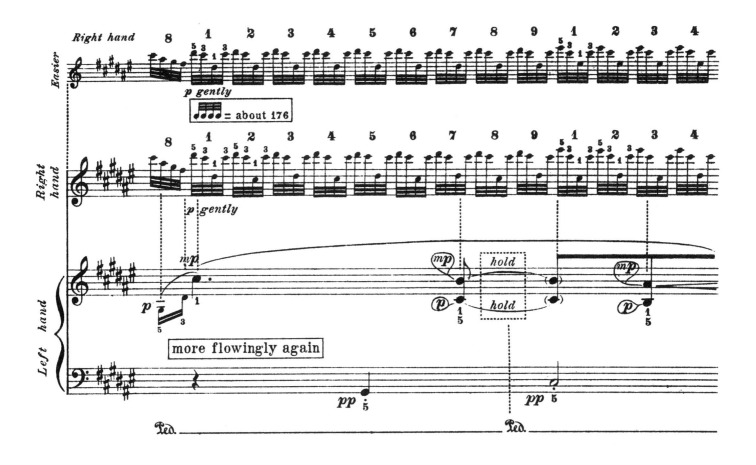

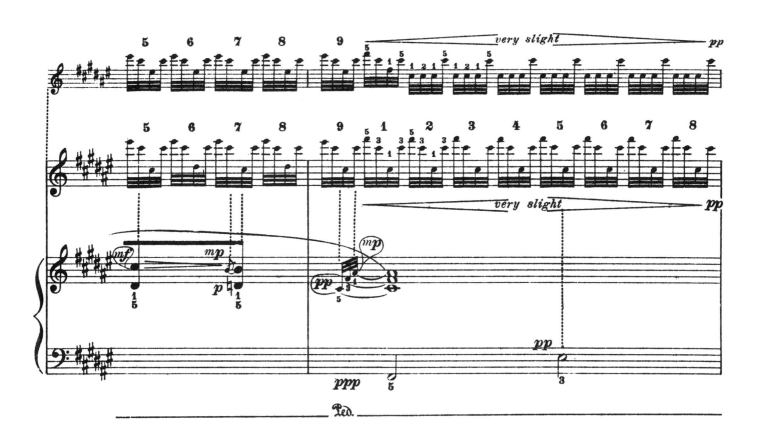

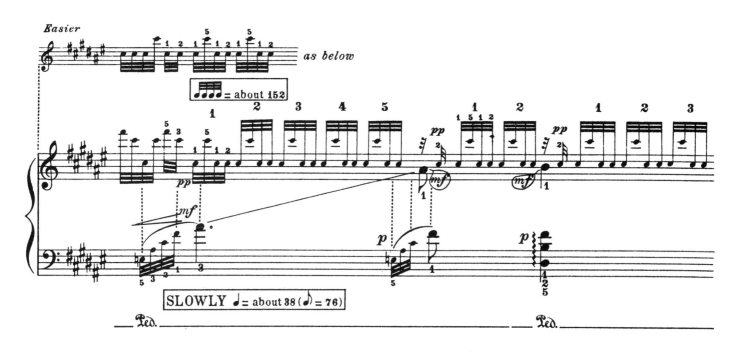

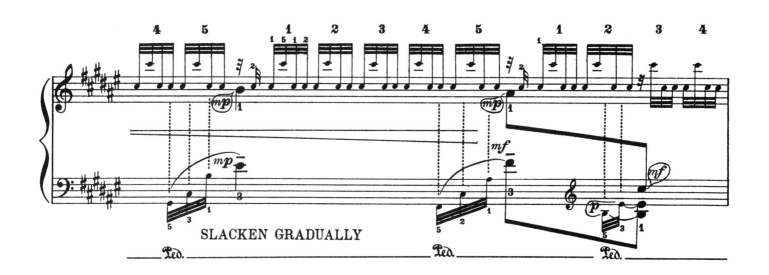

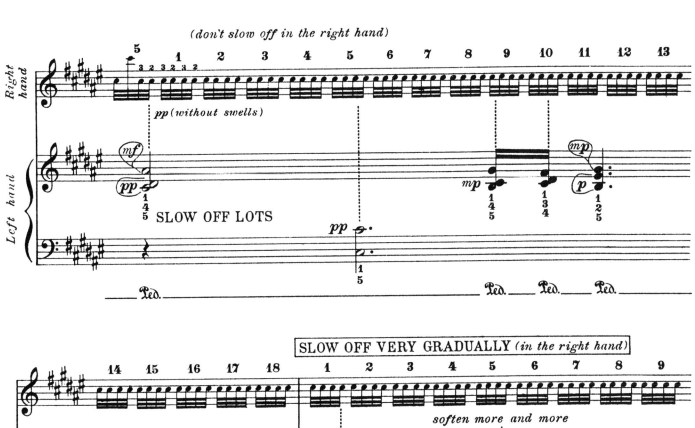

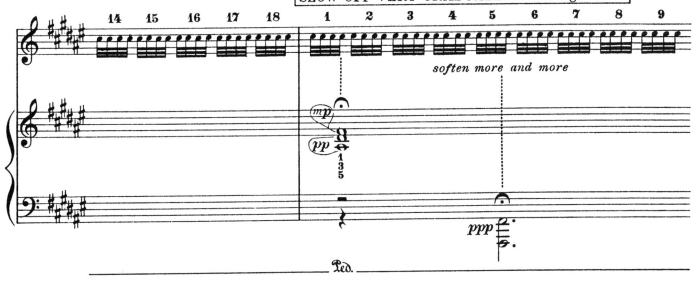

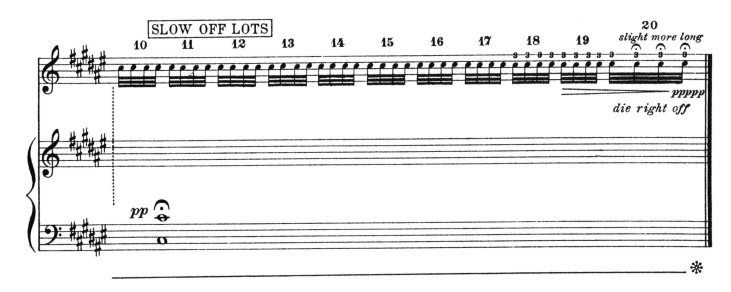

SEA-CHANTY SETTINGS
by
Percy Aldridge Grainger

N.º 1. "ONE MORE DAY, MY JOHN"

(By kind permission of Mr. Charles Rosher, C.E., F.R.G.S.)

SEA-CHANTY

from the fine collection of Mr. Charles Rosher, C. E., F. R. G. S., painter, author and collector of sea-chanties; noted down from his singing by Percy Aldridge Grainger in London in 1906, and here set in the form of a

PRELIMINARY CANTER

| short rambling prelude before starting off to play |

for Piano

by

PERCY ALDRIDGE GRAINGER.

| set fall of 1915, New York City |

The chanty as sung by Mr. Rosher ran as follows:

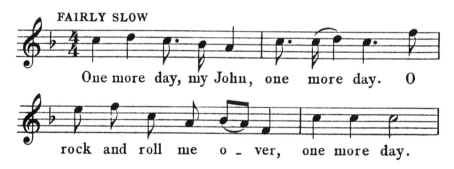

FAIRLY SLOW

One more day, my John, one more day. O
rock and roll me o _ ver, one more day.

    I find it hard to make up my mind as to how far such chanties are of British, American or Negro origin. Maybe various influences are blended in them. It will be seen that the tail-piece (starting bar 17) is a free addition of my own, as well as several twiddles.

PERCY ALDRIDGE GRAINGER.

"ONE MORE DAY, MY JOHN"

Sea-chanty

set for Piano in the form of a

Preliminary Canter

by

PERCY ALDRIDGE GRAINGER.

> **N.B.** This piece may be key-shifted (transposed) into any key so as to serve as a "preliminary canter" before any piece in any key.
>
> All big stretches may be harped (played *arpeggio*) at will.

> Lazy and dreamy, with a somewhat wafted far-away lilt.
>
> M.M. ♩ = about 63

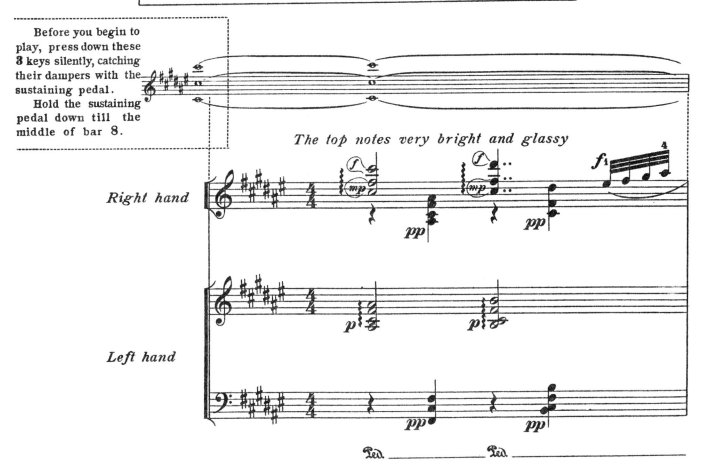

The top notes very bright and glassy

Before you begin to play, press down these **3** keys silently, catching their dampers with the sustaining pedal.

Hold the sustaining pedal down till the middle of bar 8.

Right hand

Left hand

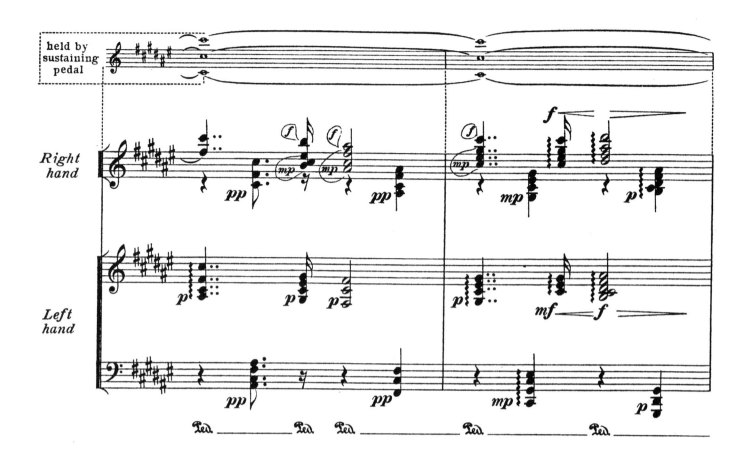

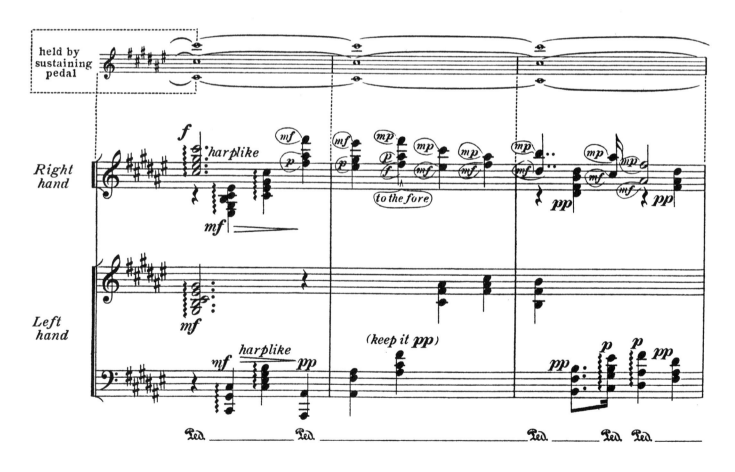

In time again

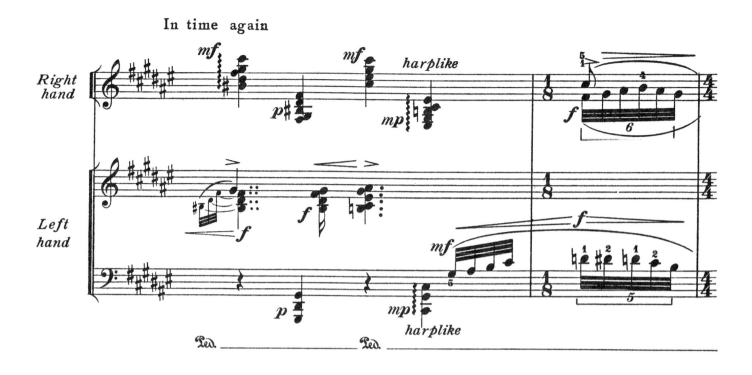

Slightly slower

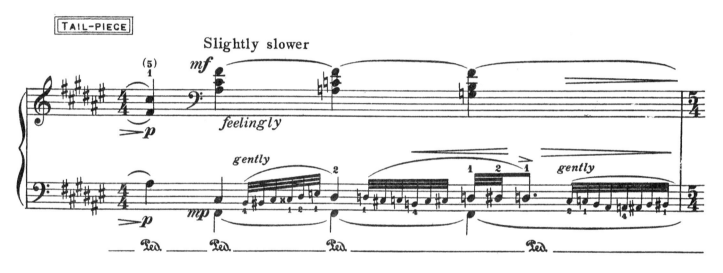

slow off   1st speed   slow off lots

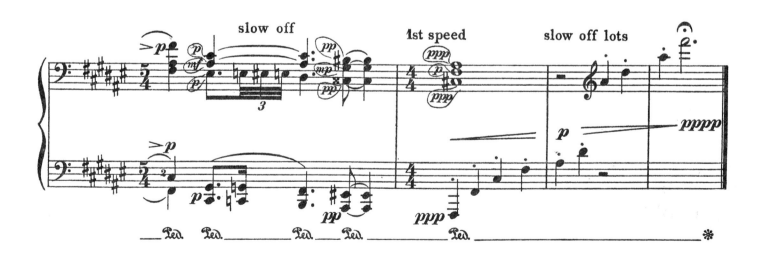

FOUR IRISH DANCES

Stanford - Grainger

The "Four Irish Dances" were originally composed for orchestra by Sir Charles Villiers Stanford, and are here freely arranged for piano by Percy Grainger. The music is based on traditional Irish folktunes selected from "The Complete Petrie Collection of Ancient Irish Music" (edited from the original manuscripts by Charles Villiers Stanford, and published by Boosey & Co., London and New York); three wonderful volumes, (containing no less than 1582 tunes and tune-variants), that should be consulted by everyone interested in folk-music in general and in Irish melodies in particular. All the tunes quoted in the following notes on the dances are reprinted from this "The Complete Petrie Collection," to which all page-numbers and tune-numbers refer.

Nº 1. A March-Jig ("Maguire's Kick")

The main tune of the March-Jig, "Maguire's Kick" by name, was used as a marching air by the Irish rebels in 1798. A county of Leitrim Jig tune is also made use of in this movement.

Tune Nº 410 (page 104)

Tune Nº 952 (page 242)

See also tunes Nºˢ 212, 409, 955, 1051

IRISH DANCES

№ 1
March-Jig ("Maguire's Kick")

*New Edition
Edited, fingered and revised
by
Percy Grainger

STANFORD - GRAINGER

*The bars between $ and $$ may be omitted.

N.º 18. "KNIGHT AND SHEPHERD'S DAUGHTER."

FOR HOWARD BROCKWAY, IN ADMIRATION

Folk-song collected in Lincolnshire, England, in 1906 by Percy Aldridge Grainger and

SET FOR PIANO BY

PERCY ALDRIDGE GRAINGER set Feb. 8-9-10, 1918

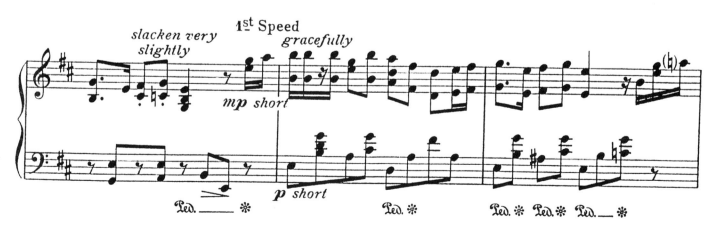

Knight and Shepherd's Daughter

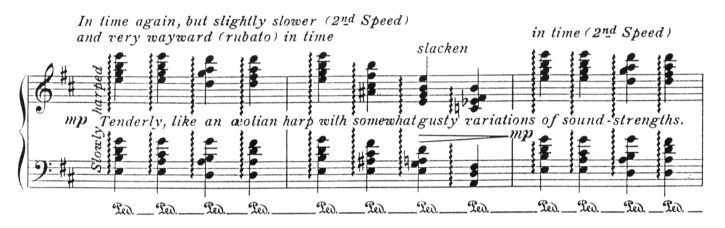

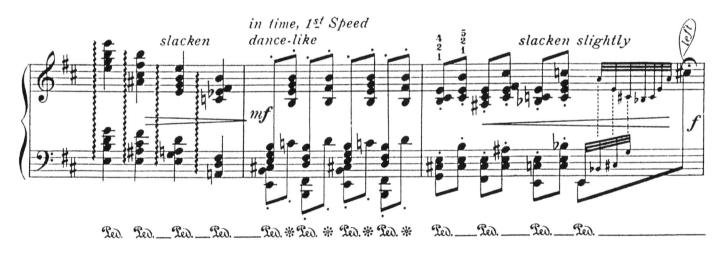

(The whole set lovingly and reverently dedicated to the memory of Edvard Grieg)

N. 22. "Country Gardens"

English Morris Dance Tune

Collected by

Cecil J. Sharp

set for piano by

PERCY ALDRIDGE GRAINGER

Playing time: 1 min., 50 sec.

Birthday gift, mother, July 3, 1918

Rough-sketched for 2 whistlers and a few instruments about 1908

Worked out for piano, spring, 1918

PROGRAM NOTE

Groups of countryside dancers—"teams" of "Morris Men"—decked out with ribbons and jingling bells, still dance the Morris Dance to the accompaniment of such tunes as "Shepherd's Hey" and "Country Gardens" in some parts of rural England. We owe our knowledge of such things to that genius among folk-music collectors, Cecil J. Sharp, and those interested in the subject should consult MORRIS DANCE TUNES and THE MORRIS BOOK, both by Cecil J. Sharp and Herbert C. Macilwaine and both published by Novello & Co., Ltd.

The traditional tune, as collected by Cecil J. Sharp, is as follows:

"Country Gardens"
Handkerchief Dance

(Morris Dance Tunes, Set 1, No. 3)

My use of the tune has very kindly been sanctioned by Mr. Cecil J. Sharp and by Novello & Co., Ltd., London.

PERCY ALDRIDGE GRAINGER
New York City, Nov., 1918.

Fairly fast (M.M. ♩ = about 92) and with a leisurely swing
The top notes louder and sharper than the rest

98

"SPOON RIVER"

American Folk-dance

The fiddle tune below was sent me by Capt. Charles H. Robinson in the summer of 1915, at my request, after he had written me in regard to *Spoon River Anthology* that he had heard the old fiddlers play this tune when he lived in Stark County, Illinois, in 1857.

Edgar Lee Masters

February 11th. 1922.

"Spoon River"
Fiddle-tune

as heard in 1857 at a dance at Bradford, Illinois, U.S.A.,
by Capt. Charles H. Robinson

Nº 1. "SPOON RIVER"

(For Edgar Lee Masters, poet of pioneers)

American folk-dance, heard played by a fiddler at a country dance at Bradford, Illinois, in 1857, by Capt. Charles H. Robinson

and set for piano by

PERCY ALDRIDGE GRAINGER

Set, March 10, 1919,
New York City, and
Jan. 29-30, 1922,
White Plains, N.Y.

Sturdily, not too fast; with "pioneer" persistency. ♩ = about 168

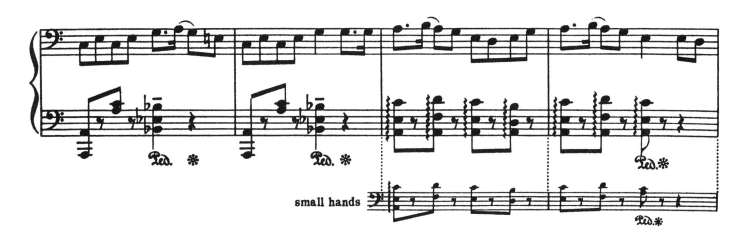

The accents as rough and heavy as possible

accents as before

(no pedal)
(small hands may break these

detached

louden hugely

chords)

fist   Top voice   Much slower   in time
        fff   (♪ = about 100) (1st speed)
                                  slacken

Written out in train, Canadian
Rockies, March 24, 1922

NATTERGALEN

Sungen af Fru Ane Nielsen Post, Gjedsø, Tem Sogn, Jylland, Danmark, d. 25de Aug., 1922. Samlet af Evald Tang Kristensen og Percy Aldridge Grainger. Nedskrevet efter Fonogrammer, d. 16de Juli, 1923.

THE NIGHTINGALE

Sung by Mrs. Ane Nielsen Post, Gjedsø, Tem Sogn, Jutland, Denmark, on Aug. 25, 1922. Gathered by Evald Tang Kristensen and Percy Aldridge Grainger. Noted down from phonograms, July 16, 1923.

1. Jeg ved vel hvor der stan-der en Slot, saa dej-lig pry-det og si-ret med Sølv og med det rø - de Guld, med

u-i-hu-ne Ste-ne op-mur-et. 2. Og ved den Slot der stan-der en Lind, med Bla-de saa dejlig og grønne, og
(udhugne)

der-ud-i boer en Nat-te-gal fin, saa lys-tig kan rø - re sin Tunge. 3. Der kom en Ridder ri - dendes frem, at
(Nattergal)

hø-re den Nat-ter-gal kvæ-de; der-ov-er han høj-lig for - und-ret sig, ti det var ved Mid-nat-tets Ti - de.

DE TO SØSTRE, eller
DE TALENDE STRENGE

Sungen af Fru Ane Nielsen Post, Gjedsø, Tem Sogn, Jylland, Danmark, d. 25de Aug., 1922. Samlet af Evald Tang Kristensen og Percy Aldridge Grainger. Nedskrevet efter Fonogrammer, d. 12te Juli, 1923.

THE TWO SISTERS

Sung by Mrs. Ane Nielsen Post, Gjedsø, Tem Sogn, Jutland, Denmark, on Aug. 25, 1922. Gathered by Evald Tang Kristensen and Percy Aldridge Grainger. Noted down from phonograms, July 12, 1923.

Der var to Søs - tr - e i__ vor Gaard, der var to Søs - tr - e i__ vor Gaard;

den en - e som Sol, den an-den som Jord. Det er saa fag-ert om Som - mer-en.

NB: On p. 113, m. 7, the first triplet—A-G-F#—is given as it appeared in Grainger's manuscript. However, both the orchestral version and the original folksong —"The Nightingale," notated above in a different key—give the triplet pitches as A-F#-E (equal to E-C#-B in the folksong transposition).

"THE NIGHTINGALE" and "THE TWO SISTERS"

PERCY ALDRIDGE GRAINGER

(1923)

Edited by Joseph Smith

"BLITHE BELLS"

BACH- GRAINGER

Set, Nov. 1930-
Feb. 1931

A free ramble by Percy Aldridge Grainger on Bach's aria "Sheep may graze in safety when a goodly shepherd watches o'er them" (from the Secular Cantata "Was mir behagt, ist nur die muntre Jagd"). The ramble is colored by the thought that Bach, in writing the melody in thirds that opens and closes the number, may have aimed at giving a hint of the sound of sheep bells.

PIANO SOLO
CONCERT VERSION